MW00565328

Originally published in a different format by Gnaana Company, LLC: ISBN 978-0-98215-991-0 (softcover).

Illustrations prepared in coordination with Kate Armstrong, Madison & Mi Design Boutique.
Text translation by Madhu Rye. Book design by Sara Petrous.

Cataloging-in-Publication Data available at the Library of Congress.

ISBN 978-1-943018-02-4

Gnaana Company, LLC
P.O. Box 10513
Fullerton, CA 92838

www.gnaana.com

Bindi Baby

by gnaana

जानवर • Jaanvar

Animals (Hindi)

ष

सुअर

suar

व

बतख
batakh

ह

हाथी

haathee

म

मेंदक

mEndak

बाघ

baagh

क

कुत्ता

kuttaa

ਤ

उल्लू

ulloo

घ

घोड़ा

ghorDaa

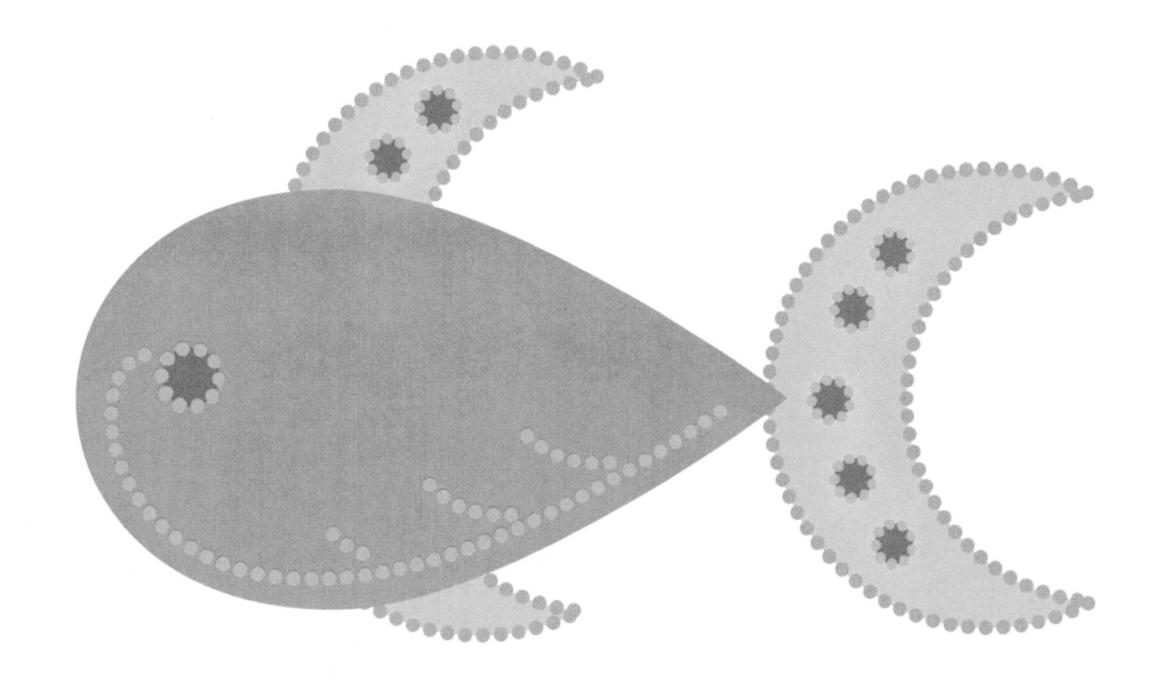

मछली

maChlee

ख

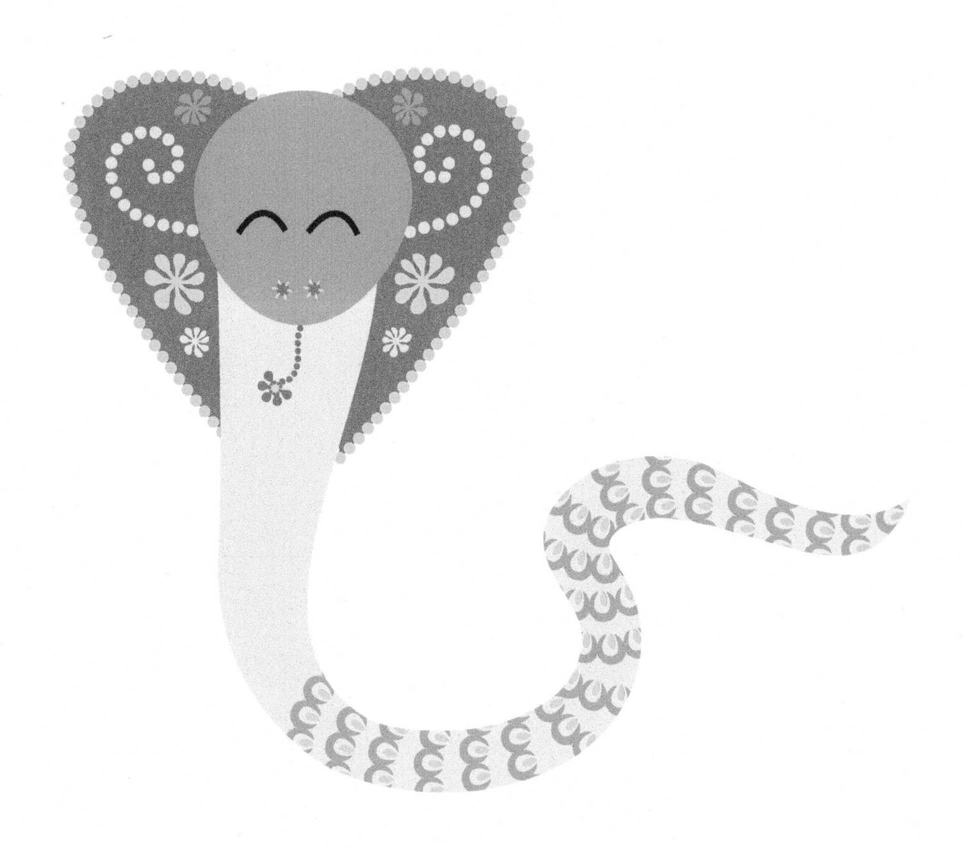

साँप
saamp

ह

हिरन

hiran

प

पक्षी

pakShee

म

मोर
mor

ग

गाय

gaay

व

बंदर

bandar

च

चूहा

choohaa

व

बिल्ली

billee

ख

खरगोश

khargosh

श